TONGA TRA\
GUIDE
FOR BEGINNERS

The Updated Concise Guide for Planning a Trip to Tonga Including Top Destinations,Culture,Outdoor Adventures,Dining,Cuisine and Getting Around

Koroth Renjar
Copyright@2023

TABLE OF CONTENT

CHAPTER 1

INTRODUCTION

Tonga, an often overlooked destination situated in the central region of the South Pacific Ocean, entices tourists with its captivating charm, unspoiled coastlines, and culturally significant Polynesian legacy. Situated inside the expansive Pacific region, this archipelagic country, often known as the "Friendly Islands," presents itself as a distinctive locale that encompasses a harmonious fusion of scenic splendor, cultural dynamism, and kind reception. This thorough travel guide focuses on the exploration of the Kingdom of Tonga, aiming to reveal its hidden aspects and provide a wealth of knowledge and insights for anyone intending to visit this tropical paradise.

A Concise Examination of the Kingdom of Tonga

Tonga, formally recognized as the Kingdom of Tonga, is an independent group of islands in Polynesia, located within the expanse of the South Pacific Ocean. The region consists of a total of 169 islands, with a mere 36 of them being populated. This characteristic renders it an alluring location for those in search of pristine environments and an authentic communion with the natural world. The land size of this island country is estimated to be about 748 square kilometers. It is geographically separated into five distinct island groups, namely Tongatapu, 'Eua, Ha'apai, Vava'u, and the Niuas. Each of these groupings has its own distinctive allure and charms.

The historical background of Tonga is deeply rooted in Polynesian cultural traditions, and it is noteworthy for being the only Pacific island country that has never experienced colonization by an external authority. The Tongan people continue to maintain a vibrant cultural legacy, which is prominently shown in their enduring traditions, language, and rituals. Tonga, characterized by a population of around 100,000 individuals, is a closely-knit society that places significant emphasis on familial bonds and the preservation of traditional values.

The objective of the travel guide is to provide comprehensive and informative content to assist travelers in planning their trips and making informed decisions.

The primary objective of this Tonga Travel Guide is to function as an extensive and all-encompassing source of information for anybody seeking to undertake a remarkable expedition to the Kingdom of Tonga. This guide aims to offer crucial information, tips, and insights to individuals embarking on a journey to Tonga, regardless of their level of travel experience. Whether one is an experienced traveler in search of unconventional experiences or a novice enticed by the appeal of unspoiled beaches and dynamic culture, this guide is tailored to ensure a pleasant and unforgettable trip.

It is acknowledged that the process of organizing a journey to a distant location such as Tonga may elicit feelings of anticipation and difficulty. Consequently, the purpose of this book is to provide important insights into several facets of travel, including transportation methods, optimal timing for visits, accommodation options, recommended activities and attractions, as well as strategies for effectively engaging with the local culture and adhering to customary practices. Furthermore, we will examine practical factors like as health and safety, transportation, and responsible travel practices in order to guarantee that your journey to Tonga is not only educational but also demonstrates respect for the local environment and cultures.

The intended recipients of this communication.

The purpose of this Tonga Travel Guide is to cater to a wide array of tourists that possess a collective inclination towards the exploration of Tonga's natural splendor and cultural heritage. The service accommodates a diverse range of individuals or groups.

1. Enthusiasts of Adventure: Individuals seeking to engage in immersive experiences within Tonga's abundant natural landscapes, including activities like as swimming in pristine seas, through verdant jungles, and exploring volcanic terrains.

2. Cultural Enthusiasts: Individuals that possess a strong interest in exploring the multifaceted Tongan culture, including traditional dances, rituals, and the amiable reception provided by the indigenous population.

3. Enthusiasts of Coastal Environments: Individuals with a strong affinity for coastal settings who are ready to indulge in the pleasures of sunbathing on unspoiled, untrodden beaches, or partake in aquatic pursuits such as kayaking, paddleboarding, and swimming.

4. Enthusiasts of History and Heritage: Individuals who are inclined towards immersing themselves in the exploration of Tonga's historical landmarks, museums, and acquiring knowledge about the captivating narratives of its bygone era.

5. Responsible Travelers: These are individuals who are dedicated to engaging in responsible and sustainable tourism activities, with the aim of reducing their environmental footprint and providing help to local communities.

6. Autonomous Travelers: Individuals who choose to design their own travel plans and navigate Tonga at their own desired speed, equipped with important knowledge and suggestions.

7. Novice Travelers: Individuals who are visiting the South Pacific area for the first time and are in need of a thorough guide

that provides assistance in handling the logistical aspects and cultural intricacies specific to Tonga.

8. Families Seeking Adventure: Families in search of activities and lodgings suitable for all members, since Tonga is a place that warmly embraces tourists of many age groups.

In the following pages, we shall explore the complexities involved in organizing a journey to Tonga, with the aim of guaranteeing a pleasurable and profoundly enlightening experience. This comprehensive book provides valuable information about visa requirements, transportation logistics, Tongan cuisine, and the tranquil beaches of the Kingdom of Tonga. It aims to provide readers with the necessary knowledge and confidence to start on an unforgettable vacation in this destination. Let us go on a voyage to collectively discover the marvels of this Polynesian paradise.

CHAPTER 2

Regions and Islands of Tonga

Tonga, a sovereign state in Polynesia, comprises a beautiful archipelago situated in the central region of the South Pacific Ocean. Tonga, a nation consisting of 169 islands, has a wide array of opportunities for exploration, including scenic coastlines, brilliant coral reefs, verdant jungles, and a culturally significant history. In this part, we will undertake a virtual exploration of Tonga's five main island clusters, each with distinctive allure and points of interest, therefore unveiling the hidden riches that lie in store for intrepid visitors in search of both excitement and tranquility.
$$$
Tongatapu is the main island of the Kingdom of Tonga, located in the South Pacific Ocean. It is the

The phrase "Gateway to the Kingdom" refers to a significant entry point or access point to a certain realm or domain.

Tongatapu, the most extensive and densely populated island within the archipelago of Tonga, serves as the primary entry point to the sovereign state. The nation of Tonga include the capital city, Nuku'alofa, which serves as a hub for vibrant marketplaces, significant historical landmarks, and the central nexus of Tonga's political and cultural affairs. Tongatapu has a diverse range of activities that are quite enjoyable.

Nuku'alofa, the capital city of Tonga, serves as the political, economic, and cultural center of the nation.

Vibrant Markets: Commence your Tongan expedition by embarking on an exploration of the lively Talamahu Market in Nuku'alofa. This busy marketplace serves as a gathering place for residents to engage in the trade of fresh agricultural products, handicrafts, and apparel. This location offers an excellent opportunity for anyone to fully engage with and experience the customs, traditions, and way of life of the indigenous population.

The Royal Palace is a notable architectural landmark constructed in the 1860s, characterized by its impressive timber construction. Although access to the palace inside is restricted, one may still appreciate the elaborate architectural design and exquisite gardens from its outside.

The Centenary Church is a renowned historical site, celebrated for its unique architectural design and significance as a religious sanctuary for Tonga's royal family.

The B. Ha'amonga 'a Maui Trilithon is a significant archaeological site located in Tonga.

The Ha'amonga 'a Maui Trilithon, often known as the Stonehenge of the Pacific, is an ancient monument that may be seen. The origins of this antiquated stone edifice, with an estimated mass of around 40 metric tons, are thought to date back to the 13th century. Its construction is regarded as a remarkable spectacle.

C. 'Eua Island: An Idyllic Destination for Nature Enthusiasts

The island of 'Eua, situated in close proximity to Tongatapu, has several prospects for adventure and nature enthusiasts, including engaging in activities like as hiking, horseback riding, and bird-watching. The presence of spectacular cliffs, rich woods, and distinctive flora and wildlife makes it an ideal sanctuary for those with a keen interest in the natural world.

The topic of discussion is the island of 'Eua.

The Unspoiled Wilderness

The island of 'Eua, located in the southern region of Tonga, is sometimes characterized as a "unspoiled wilderness" owing to its steep topography and pristine aesthetic. This destination serves as a sanctuary for those who are enthusiastic about embarking on thrilling experiences and have a deep appreciation for the natural world.

The topic of discussion pertains to hiking trails.

The Cross-Island Track is a demanding hiking trail that spans the whole of 'Eua, including its verdant rainforests, imposing cliffs, and providing awe-inspiring vistas of the island. This full-day excursion provides a rigorous physical experience for outdoor enthusiasts seeking to immerse themselves in the natural beauty of the region.

The Tumu'a Mountain, which stands as the highest peak in 'Eua, offers a remarkable opportunity to ascend and get a unique perspective of the island and its surrounding seas.

B. Distinctive Fauna

Bird-watching enthusiasts will find 'Eua to be an ideal destination, as it offers a plethora of opportunities to see various avian species that are exclusive to the region. Notably, the 'Eua Kingfisher and the Koki parrot are among the unique birds that can be found in this paradise for bird-watchers.

Natural caves are geological formations that are formed over thousands or millions of years by various natural processes. These caves are often found in areas with limestone or other soluble rocks, including

One may engage in the exploration of natural caves in 'Eua, such as the 'Anahulu Cave, which is renowned for its underground ponds and limestone formations.

The topic of discussion is Ha'apai.

The location being described may be characterized as a tranquil tropical haven.

The archipelago of Ha'apai, situated in the central region of Tonga, has a total of 62 islands, with a mere 17 of them being populated. The Ha'apai region is a calm tropical haven that appeals to anyone in search of serenity and unspoiled natural surroundings.

One notable aspect of the location is the presence of stunning beaches.

Pangai Beach offers a serene environment for those seeking relaxation, including a picturesque expanse of pristine white sand that beckons visitors to engage in activities like as swimming, sunbathing, or leisurely walks along the shoreline.

B. The Activities of Snorkeling and Diving

Ha'apai is renowned for its exceptional snorkeling and diving opportunities, offering access to remarkable coral reefs teeming with a vast array of marine organisms, such as vivid fish species and sea turtles.

C. Observing Humpback Whales

During the whale season, it is highly recommended to take advantage of the chance to engage in humpback whale watching, particularly if you plan to travel between the months of June and October.

The Ha'apai region serves as an ideal destination for seeing these magnificent animals during their migration to the temperate seas of Tonga for the purposes of reproduction and mating.

Vava'u is an archipelago located in the Kingdom of Tonga in the South Pacific Ocean.

The topic of discussion pertains to the concept of "Sailing Paradise and Aquatic Adventure."

Vava'u, located in the northern region of Tonga, is an idyllic destination that has great appeal for sailors and serves as a haven for anyone seeking aquatic adventures. Vava'u has a diverse array of captivating activities, owing to its well-protected ports, islands adorned with coral formations, and pristine seas of exceptional clarity.

Sailing and yachting are recreational activities that include the use of sailboats and yachts for navigation on bodies of water. These activities are popular among those who seek leisure and adventure on the open seas.$$$

Vava'u Harbor, located near Neiafu, is renowned for its scenic beauty and serves as a central gathering point for sailors and boat enthusiasts. One has the option to engage in yacht chartering as a means of exploring the neighboring islands and experiencing the liberating sensation of traversing the vast expanse of the open sea.

Swimming with cetaceans, namely whales, is a topic of interest that warrants academic study.

The region of Vava'u is well recognized for its exceptional prospects to engage in swimming activities with humpback whales during their reproductive period. This remarkable encounter provides everyone with the opportunity to closely see these docile behemoths in their own environment.

C. Mariner's Cave is a notable geological formation that has significance due to its unique characteristics and historical relevance.

Cave Exploration: Delve into the depths of Mariner's Cave, an extraordinary subaquatic cavern that may be accessed by traversing a slender passageway across the water. Upon entering, one will be welcomed by a surreal and brilliantly lit cavern.

The Niuas are a group of islands located in the Pacific Ocean.

The Concept of Remote and Untouched Beauty

The Niuas, which consist of the islands of Niuafo'ou, Niuatoputapu, and Tafahi, are geographically situated as the northernmost and most isolated islands within the nation of Tonga. In this location, individuals have the opportunity to immerse themselves in unspoiled natural landscapes and cultivate a genuine feeling of seclusion.

A. Niuafo'ou: The Island Known as the "Tin Can Island"

Niuafo'ou, an island of volcanic origin, has a distinctive geographical characteristic that distinguishes it from other landforms. Historically referred to as the "Tin Can Island," this appellation stemmed from its remote location and the unconventional method used for mail delivery, including the use of sealed cans propelled by cannons.

Niuafo'ou, despite its volcanic genesis, exhibits a captivating amalgamation of severe topography and innate beauty, characterized by its verdant foliage.

B. Niuatoputapu: An Island Inhabited by Hospitable Residents

Niuatoputapu is renowned for its amicable residents who often offer cordial invites to guests, inviting them to partake in communal feasts and cultural gatherings.

The subject of this study is the remote volcanic peak known as C. Tafahi.

The island of Tafahi offers an opportunity for anyone seeking adventure to engage in a volcanic expedition. This entails embarking on a walk to its volcanic summit, which rewards participants with breathtaking panoramic vistas of the surrounding seascape.

The nation of Tonga has a variety of regions and islands that provide a wide range of activities, including opportunities for cultural immersion, outdoor excursions, and tranquil leisure. Each destination in Tonga offers a distinct and memorable journey, whether it be exploring the lively capital of Tongatapu, trekking the challenging trails of 'Eua, immersing oneself in the vibrant underwater realm of Ha'apai, sailing the picturesque waters of Vava'u, or uncovering the remote splendor of The Niuas. In the following chapters, a comprehensive exploration of each place will be conducted, providing readers with the necessary insights and knowledge to meticulously design their ideal expedition inside this Polynesian utopia.

CHAPTER 3

Things to Do and See in Tonga

Tonga, colloquially known as the "Friendly Islands," is a tropical destination situated in the South Pacific region. It has a diverse range of activities and attractions, catering to the preferences of tourists seeking adventure, leisure, and cultural engagement. Tonga has a diverse range of attractions, including unspoiled beaches, translucent seas, immersive cultural encounters, and exhilarating outdoor pursuits, catering to the preferences of many categories of explorers. This section will examine the wide range of activities and attractions available for exploration in this captivating realm.

One of the most popular recreational destinations for tourists and locals alike are beaches, which provide a wide range of water activities.

The coastal region of Tonga has a remarkable and aesthetically pleasing landscape, characterized by the presence of very scenic and pristine beaches that are renowned globally. Regardless of one's preference for beachcombing or engaging in water sports, there are a wide range of activities available to cater to diverse interests.

Anahulu Beach, located on the island of Tongatapu, is a notable coastal area that attracts visitors due to its scenic beauty and recreational opportunities.

Relaxation is often sought at Anahulu Beach located on the island of Tongatapu, where people engage in sunbathing, picnics, and leisurely swims among the tranquil, blue waters.

B. Ha'atafu Beach, located on the island of Tongatapu, is a notable coastal area that warrants academic attention.

Surfing at Ha'atafu Beach, located on the island of Tongatapu, is renowned for its exceptional surfing opportunities, particularly during the winter season. Both novice and expert surfers have the opportunity to ride remarkable waves at this location.

C. Snorkeling and Diving in the Ha'apai and Vava'u Regions

The regions of Ha'apai and Vava'u are well recognized for their exceptional coral reefs, characterized by their vivid colors and rich biodiversity of marine organisms. Participants are encouraged to equip themselves with snorkeling gear or engage in scuba diving in order to investigate and appreciate the remarkable aquatic ecosystem present in this submerged paradise.

In the region of Vava'u, two popular water activities are kayaking and paddleboarding.

The calm and protected waters of Vava'u provide an ideal environment for engaging in activities like as kayaking and paddleboarding. Navigate across isolated bays, inlets, and concealed shorelines by means of paddling.

2. Locations for Snorkeling and Diving

Tonga is widely regarded as a popular destination for anyone with a keen interest in underwater activities, as it provides a unique opportunity to see a diverse array of marine life and vibrant coral reefs within the context of pristine, temperate seas.

One notable location in Vava'u is Swallows Cave.

The Swallows Cave in Vava'u offers a unique opportunity for cave diving, allowing divers to explore an underwater tunnel characterized by its vivid coral formations and diverse fish population. The interplay of sunlight through the mouth of the cave gives rise to a captivating aquatic show. $$$

The B. Fafa Island Marine Reserve, located near Tongatapu, is a significant ecological area that has been designated for the protection and conservation of marine life.

The Fafa Island Marine Reserve, located near Tongatapu, offers an opportunity to investigate a diverse range of marine animals, including as turtles and rays. The act of snorkeling in this location offers a tranquil and very engaging encounter.

C. Mounu Island, located in the Vava'u region, is the subject of discussion.

Mounu Island in Vava'u is well recognized as a prominent destination for engaging in close interactions with humpback whales during their calving season. Observing these magnificent animals in close proximity is an extraordinary and unique encounter that occurs just once in a person's lifetime.

3. Cultural Experiences and Historical Sites are significant aspects of a region's heritage and provide valuable insights into its history and traditions.

The cultural heritage and historical significance of Tonga are commemorated via a diverse range of cultural encounters and notable historical landmarks.

Tongan Cultural Shows in Tongatapu

Dance and music enthusiasts have the opportunity to see traditional Tongan cultural acts, which include dynamic dances, beautiful melodies, and elaborate costumes that serve as narratives of Tongan history.

The B. Royal Palace, located in Tongatapu, is a significant architectural structure of historical and cultural importance.

The Royal Palace at Nuku'alofa, Tongatapu, serves as a significant historic landmark that offers visitors the opportunity to appreciate its elaborate architectural design while gaining insights into the rich royal history of Tonga.

The topic of discussion is ancient monuments located on the island of Tongatapu.

The Ha'amonga 'a Maui Trilithon is a notable archaeological site, recognized as the "Stonehenge of the Pacific," that originated in the 13th century. It is recommended to visit and explore this ancient stone building known as Ha'amonga 'a Maui.

The D. Langi Tombs located in Tongatapu are of significant academic interest.

The Royal Burial Ground is a significant site that houses the Langi Tombs, which are imposing stone burial mounds that have been designated as the last resting place for the esteemed monarchs and nobility of Tonga's bygone eras.

4. The Pursuit of Hiking and Outdoor Experiences

Tonga's verdant landscapes and challenging topography provide many prospects for anyone with a penchant for outdoor activities.

The Cross-Island Track on the island of 'Eua is a popular hiking trail that traverses the island from east to west.

The Cross-Island Track in 'Eua is an opportunity for an adventurous journey, including a whole day of traversing through jungles, beside high cliffs, and providing awe-inspiring panoramic vistas.

B. Tumu'a Mountain, also known as 'Eua, is a prominent geographical feature that has significance in academic discourse.

Embark on a challenging expedition to ascend Tumu'a Mountain in 'Eua, the highest summit on the island, in order to get a gratifying perspective that affords panoramic views of the surrounding island and vast ocean.

C. The Activity of Kayaking at the Island of 'Eua

Coastal Exploration: Engage in the exploration of 'Eua's unspoiled coastline via the use of kayaks, hence facilitating access to concealed coves and caves.

Mount Talau, located in the Vava'u region, is a prominent geographical feature.

One may ascend Mount Talau in Vava'u to see breathtaking panoramic vistas of the encompassing islands and ocean.

In this section, we will discuss the topic of wildlife and nature reserves.

Tonga's varied ecosystems provide prospects for engaging with the natural environment and seeing distinctive fauna.

Bird-Watching at 'Eua Island

The island of 'Eua offers a favorable environment for bird enthusiasts, since it provides enough opportunity to see avian species that are unique to the region, such as the 'Eua Kingfisher and the Koki parrot.

B. Observing Humpback Whales in the Ha'apai and Vava'u Regions

The phenomenon of majestic migrations may be seen in the case of humpback whales as they undertake their annual journey to the warm seas of Tonga throughout the period spanning from June to October. The islands of Ha'apai and Vava'u are considered to be exceptional destinations for anyone seeking a really remarkable and captivating encounter.

The topic of interest is the hatching of turtles at C. Keleti Beach in Vava'u.

Sea turtle conservation may be seen at Keleti Beach in Vava'u, where the nesting and hatching of sea turtles can be witnessed. There are ongoing local initiatives that are directed towards the protection and conservation of these remarkable species.

6. Workshops on Tapa Making and Craft

Explore the richness of Tongan culture via engaging in workshops and watching the intricate craft-making processes that have been passed down through generations.

A. Tapa Production in Tongatapu

Cultural Art: Engage in a Tapa making session in Tongatapu, which offers an opportunity to acquire knowledge about the customary practice of crafting Tapa fabric from mulberry bark.

B. Handicrafts in Tonga
Artisan Souvenirs: Engage in an exploration of local markets and stores around Tonga in order to get handmade souvenirs, including a diverse range of

items such as wood carvings, woven baskets, and jewelry.

7. The Tradition of Feasting and Tongan Culinary Culture

Indulge in the diverse and delectable tastes of Tongan cuisine, renowned for its use of locally sourced fish and an array of tropical ingredients.

The 'Umu Feast, which is celebrated across Tonga, is a significant cultural event in the country.

The traditional banquet offers participants the opportunity to partake in a 'Umu feast, a culinary event characterized by the cooking of food in an underground oven. Partaking in Tongan food is a social and delectable experience.

In this study, the focus is on the botanical characteristics and culinary uses of B. Lu, often known as Taro Leaves.

One notable culinary offering is Lu, a traditional Tongan delicacy prepared by combining taro leaves with coconut cream, often served alongside yam and pig.
C. Availability of Fresh Seafood in Tonga

Ocean Bounty offers a diverse selection of freshly sourced seafood, including a range of species such as fish, octopus, and lobster, meticulously cooked using a multitude of traditional Tongan culinary techniques.
$$$
8. Participation in Community Festivals and Events

One may enhance their cultural experience in Tonga by actively engaging in local festivals and activities.

The Heilala Festival, held on the island of Tongatapu, is a significant cultural event in the region.

The Heilala Festival in Tongatapu is a month-long commemoration that showcases various cultural performances, beauty pageants, and traditional sports, all aimed at celebrating the rich heritage of Tonga.

The B. Tupakapakanava Music Festival, held in Vava'u, is an annual event that showcases a diverse range of musical performances.
The Tupakapakanava song Festival in Vava'u offers an opportunity to immerse

oneself in the rich heritage of Tongan song, dance, and culture.

The C. Tātātu Music Festival, held in Ha'apai, is a notable event in the region.

The Tātātu Music Festival in Ha'apai is a vibrant occasion that commemorates the musical abilities of the local and regional community.

Tonga's copious natural splendor, dynamic cultural milieu, and exhilarating array of activities make it a very desirable locale for tourists in pursuit of a multifaceted and fulfilling sojourn. Tonga has a diverse range of activities and experiences for visitors to engage in. These include leisurely pursuits such as enjoying the unspoiled beaches, delving into the depths of the undersea realm, embarking on invigorating hikes among verdant woods, immersing oneself in the rich tapestry of Tongan culture, and seeing the awe-inspiring animals. A sojourn in Tonga promises an indelible and treasured voyage through this idyllic Polynesian haven.

CHAPTER 4

Tongan Culture and Etiquette

Tonga, also known as the "Friendly Islands," is a country deeply rooted in Polynesian culture and customs. The amicable and hospitable disposition shown by the Tongan populace is a distinctive attribute of the sovereign state, hence necessitating visitors to possess comprehension and reverence for the indigenous traditions and protocols. This section aims to explore the many aspects of Tongan culture, providing an in-depth analysis of the traditions, social standards, and etiquettes that influence daily life in this Polynesian archipelago.

One significant aspect of human social organization is the concept of family and community.

Tongan culture is characterized by the presence of strong familial and communal ties. The significance of these relationships is of paramount importance in the lives of those belonging to the Tongan community, and is seen in several facets of their cultural practices.

The concept of respecting elders is deeply ingrained in many cultures throughout the world. It is a fundamental aspect of social norms and values, emphasizing the need of showing deference and reverence towards older individuals. This practice

The notion of "fahu" places significant emphasis on the need of demonstrating reverence for those of advanced age. In the cultural context of Tonga, it is normal to adhere to a social protocol that involves greeting and acknowledging elder folks prior to initiating any kind of discussion or engagement in activities.

In the context of social gatherings or events, it is customary for younger persons to occupy seats towards the rear as a means of displaying deference and reverence for their older counterparts.

B. Extended Families

In the context of Faka-Tokelau, it is observed that Tongan families tend to exhibit characteristics of being both big and extended. The concept of "faka-Tokelau" pertains to the customary tradition of inviting and accommodating not only immediate family members but also others from the extended family and close social circles into one's household.

Communal Meals: The act of partaking in shared meals is a prevalent practice among Tongans, serving as a means to reinforce familial ties and foster social relationships. As a gesture of hospitality, visitors may be extended invitations to participate in community meals.

2. Salutations and Interpersonal Interaction

Communication in Tonga is distinguished by a kind and deferential demeanor. A comprehensive grasp of the subtleties associated with welcomes and exchanges has significant importance for those who are visiting a particular place.

In this section, we will discuss traditional greetings.

The usual salutation in Tonga is "Mālō e lelei," which translates to "Hello" or "Good day." The use of this expression during interactions with individuals from the local community is highly regarded and serves as an indication of courteousness.

Gestures of Greeting: The act of shaking hands is a prevalent method of greeting, sometimes accompanied by a facial expression known as a grin. Maintaining eye contact is considered crucial in interpersonal communication as it serves as a nonverbal indicator of respect.

The topic of language is of great importance in the field of linguistics. Language is a complex and dynamic system of communication that is

The Tongan language serves as the official language of Tonga, however it is worth noting that a significant number of Tongans are also fluent in English. Acquiring rudimentary Tongan expressions, such as "Mālō" (expressing gratitude) and "'Ofa atu" (conveying affection), may significantly contribute to fostering interpersonal connections.

The use of appropriate titles, such as "Siaosi" for a male person called George or "Kalolaine" for a female individual named Caroline, is indicative of a respectful gesture.

The third topic of discussion pertains to clothing and the establishment of a dress code.

Tongan attire exhibits a fusion of customary and Western elements. Having knowledge of the suitable clothing for various events is crucial.

The concept of "Sunday Best" refers to the practice of dressing in one's finest attire on Sundays, particularly for religious services or other formal occasions. This tradition has historical

Sundays in Tonga are of great religious significance, since they are dedicated to observing the Sabbath and entail the cessation of most activity. The local population often adorns themselves in formal attire, commonly referred to as their "Sunday best," while attending religious gatherings. Women choose for sophisticated outfits, while males choose to wear suits or adhere to the customary practice of donning ta'ovala, which are waist mats with cultural significance.
$$$
B. The Concept of Modesty

Swimwear is generally seen appropriate for beach settings, but it is considered disrespectful to don such gear in public spaces or while not actively participating in aquatic pursuits.

Appropriate Attire in Traditional Communities: It is recommended to don attire that adheres to modest standards, including the coverage of shoulders and knees, as an expression of deference towards indigenous cultural practices, particularly while engaging with rural communities.

In this section, we will discuss the cultural practices of gift-giving and hospitality.

The hospitality of the Tongan people is well recognized, and the act of gift-giving is a prevalent custom that serves to convey appreciation and foster interpersonal connections.

The first section of the event was the presentation of gifts.

The cultural practice of exchanging presents, referred to as "koloa," has significant value and is well rooted in history. When visiting someone's house, it is usual to provide a gift, which may include items such as a handmade mat or food.

The act of gift wrapping has cultural significance when a fahu (cloth) is used to adorn the gift during presentation.

B. Receiving Gifts

Adopting a Dual-Handed Approach: In the context of gift exchange, it is considered a courteous practice to receive a present by use both hands, therefore expressing gratitude and acknowledging the act of giving.

Delayed Unveiling: It is customary for presents to be unveiled at a later time, in a more secluded setting, rather than being promptly opened upon reception.

5. The Role of the Church and Religion

Religion has a significant presence within Tongan culture, since Christianity, particularly the Free Wesleyan Church of Tonga, is widely observed by the majority of the people.

The topic of church attendance is of significant interest and has been widely studied in several academic disciplines.

Adherence to Service Etiquette: In the context of attending a church service, it is advisable to ensure punctuality and adhere to a modest dress code. In religious settings, it is a normal practice for individuals to rise from their seated positions at the entrance of a minister or pastor into the church.

Monetary Offerings: It is customary for visitors to be requested to make a monetary contribution throughout the course of the ceremony. This is a fantastic occasion to make a meaningful contribution to the immediate community.

B. Sundays

The Significance of Quiet Sundays: As previously stated, Sundays are traditionally recognized as a designated day for relaxation and religious observance. In adherence to this custom, noise levels and leisure activities are often restricted.

6. Otuhaka, also known as ceremonial events,

Tonga is renowned for its ceremonial occasions, often characterized by the inclusion of traditional dance, music, and elaborate feasting. Enhancing the cultural experience of visitors is contingent upon comprehending the importance of these events.

The Kava Ceremony is a traditional ritual used in several Pacific Island cultures.

Traditional Beverage: The kava ritual encompasses the process of preparing and communally consuming kava, a customary Polynesian beverage derived from the root of the kava plant. The object in question serves as a representation of both unity and welcome.

Culturally Appropriate Engagement: In the context of kava consumption, it is usual to demonstrate respect by clapping once before and after accepting the bowl.

The Tau'olunga dance is a traditional kind of dance originating from the Polynesian island of Tonga. It is characterized by graceful and fluid movements, often performed

The tau'olunga is a traditional dance characterized by its elegance and is often performed by young females at significant events. The aforementioned phenomenon serves as a manifestation of aesthetic appeal and the preservation of cultural legacy.

The concept of 'Otua, which pertains to the reverence and deference towards the divine, has significant importance in many cultural and religious contexts. It encompasses the recognition and acknowledgement of the divine's supreme authority and power, as well as the adherence to prescribed rituals and practices that demonstrate respect

The culture of Tonga has a notable focus on spirituality and reverence for the almighty.

A. The Role of 'Otua in Everyday Life

Spiritual Foundation: The Tongan people often incorporate religious practices into their everyday routines, actively engaging in prayer and making sacrifices as a means to seek blessings and direction from the almighty.

The Tradition of Grace Before Meals: It is a usual practice to engage in a prayer of thanksgiving before and after meals as a means of expressing appreciation.

B. 'Otua as a Cultural Value

Respect: It is essential for visitors to have a deep understanding of the significance of 'Otua within Tongan culture and exhibit reverence towards religious rites and practices.

8. Tipping and Payment In this section, we will discuss the practices of tipping and payment.

Tonga exhibits distinct cultural practices pertaining to gratuity and financial transactions.

A. Tipping Etiquette in Various Settings

Expected: Tipping is not a prevalent custom in Tonga. In some dining establishments and lodging facilities, it is possible for service charges to be included into the final invoice.

Expression of Appreciation: In the event that you want to convey your gratitude for outstanding service, it is possible to do so via direct communication instead of relying just on monetary gratuity.

B. Methods of Payment

Cash is often regarded as the most commonly used form of payment for the majority of transactions in Tonga. Certain institutions, especially those located in more populous urban areas, have the capability to process payments made using credit cards.

Gaining knowledge and demonstrating reverence for Tongan culture and etiquette serves as an indication of gratitude for the kind reception one is likely to experience, while also facilitating a more profound engagement with the diverse cultural fabric of this Polynesian haven. By adopting and incorporating these cultural practices and rituals, individuals have the opportunity to establish significant interpersonal relationships with the indigenous population and cultivate enduring recollections of their expedition throughout the amicable archipelago.

CHAPTER 5

Food and Dining in Tonga

Tonga, an island located in the South Pacific, is renowned for its serene environment, stunning natural scenery, rich cultural heritage, and a gastronomic scene that is sure to captivate the senses. Tongan cuisine is a manifestation of the country's Polynesian lineage and the bountiful tropical resources it has. It encompasses a diverse range of freshly sourced seafood, tropical fruits, and distinctive culinary creations that are certain to captivate one's palate. In the next part, we will start a gastronomic exploration of Tonga, delving into the diverse range of tastes, customary eating practices, and indigenous culinary creations that make this sovereign state an ideal destination for lovers of fine cuisine.

1. Tongan Cuisine: An Integration of Diverse Flavors

Tongan cuisine is characterized by a harmonious amalgamation of indigenous Polynesian tastes, elements derived from nearby Pacific islands, and a subtle incorporation of Western culinary influences. The culinary offerings are renowned for their emphasis on minimalism, quality, and the use of regionally procured components. The following are essential components of Tongan gastronomy:

The first category of seafood that will be discussed is fresh seafood.

Tonga, situated in the South Pacific, has a rich variety of fish species, such as tuna, mahi-mahi, and snapper, due to its favorable geographical position. Fish, whether grilled, poached, or prepared in coconut milk, is a fundamental component of the human diet.

Octopus and squid are often used in Tongan culinary practices, typically prepared by grilling or simmering in a flavorful coconut-based sauce.

B. The Role of Root Vegetables and Taro in Culinary Practices

Taro, often referred to as "talo" in the Tongan language, is a kind of starchy root vegetable that has significant importance as a food staple. Taro, a versatile ingredient, finds use in a range of culinary preparations, including taro chips, taro pudding, and the traditional meal of taro leaves cooked in coconut cream, known as lu.

The yam is a widely consumed root vegetable that is often prepared by roasting or boiling methods.

The topic of discussion is the coconut, specifically referred to as C. Coconut.

Coconut cream has a significant role as a foundational component in the culinary practices of Tonga. It is often used to enhance the palatability and gustatory experience of many culinary preparations, including curries and traditional confections originating from the Tongan culture.

Coconut water, derived from the juice of young coconuts, is widely consumed as a popular beverage, serving as an effective means of hydration in Tonga's warm climate.

Tropical fruits are a category of fruits that are often grown in tropical regions. These fruits are known for their vibrant colors, unique flavors, and nutritional benefits. Examples of

The pineapple, often consumed in its raw form or as a juice, is a delectable fruit characterized by its sweet and acidic flavor profile.

Mangoes are readily available in Tonga throughout the ripening season and are consumed in their fully ripened and succulent form.

Papaya, often referred to as "mele kivalu" in the local context, is a tropical fruit that is commonly enjoyed as a revitalizing choice for breakfast.

One aspect that sets this product apart is its distinctive flavor profiles.

The meal known as 'Ota 'ika is a customary Tongan culinary preparation that showcases the use of uncooked fish, often tuna, which is marinated in a mixture of coconut milk, lime juice, and onions. This combination of ingredients yields a delightful and invigorating taste profile characterized by its refreshing and tangy qualities.

Lu is a traditional dish consisting of taro leaves that are cooked in coconut cream, sometimes accompanied by onions and occasionally supplemented with meat or fish. The meal in question has a smooth and rich texture, with a flavor profile that is both savory and indulgent.

Feke (Octopus): Feke, often prepared by grilling, tenderizing, or stewing, is commonly served with a delectable sauce comprising coconut cream, onions, and a blend of spices.

2. Dining Experiences and Etiquette In this section, we will explore the topic of dining experiences and etiquette.

Tongan culinary encounters include more than just gastronomic indulgence, serving as a manifestation of the culture's conviviality and collective ethos. This is a brief overview of the eating experience in Tonga:

A. Fakamālō (Thank You)

Expression of thanks: Tongan people are well recognized for their notable display of graciousness, whereby the act of expressing thanks has significant value. This appreciation is conveyed via both verbal communication and non-verbal cues. It is common to express gratitude by saying "Mālō" after the consumption of a meal.

B. Family-Style Dining refers to a dining arrangement where food is served in large portions and shared among those seated at the same table.

community Meals: The Tongan culture often engages in the practice of community meals, particularly in the context of family gatherings or significant events. The act of placing dishes in the middle and allowing individuals to serve themselves is a common practice.

The 'Umu, also known as the Underground Oven, is a traditional cooking method used by several Polynesian cultures.

The 'umu is a traditional Tongan feast characterized by the cooking of food in a subterranean oven. The occasion often entails the gathering of family and friends in a communal setting.
$$$
Culinary Technique: Diverse ingredients such as taro, yam, meats, and fish are encased inside banana leaves and positioned atop heated stones within the subterranean cooking apparatus. The gradual and prolonged cooking method infuses a distinctive taste into the culinary preparations.

In this section, we will discuss the practice of sharing kava, a traditional beverage used in several cultures.

The Kava Ceremony has great cultural importance in Tonga, since it involves the use of kava, a traditional beverage derived from the root of the kava plant, which is native to Polynesia. It is often disseminated at communal meetings and ceremonial occasions.

Etiquette: In the context of a kava ceremony, there exists a prescribed set of customs and practices, sometimes referred to as protocol, which governs the proceedings. One such custom is the act of clapping, both before to and subsequent to the reception of the kava bowl, serving as a symbolic gesture denoting reverence and deference.

3. Tongan Culinary Delights Worth Exploring

To fully immerse oneself in the culinary traditions of Tonga, it is essential to sample a selection of the nation's distinctive gastronomic offerings. Presented here are few Tongan delicacies that are highly recommended for exploration and enjoyment.

The individual referred to as "A. Lu Sipi"

Description: Lu sipi is a delectable culinary creation originating from Tonga, consisting of mutton (or sometimes beef) and taro leaves that are meticulously prepared and simmered in a rich coconut cream. The dish is characterized by its rich and velvety texture.

The subject of discussion is 'Otai.

Description: Otai is a traditional beverage originating from Tonga, consisting of a blend of coconut water, watermelon or mango, and a little amount of sugar for added sweetness. This beverage serves as an ideal solution for quenching one's thirst during periods of high temperatures.

C. Feke Tukuni, often known as Octopus Salad, is a dish that is often enjoyed in several culinary traditions.

Description: Feke tukuni is a delectable salad that has octopus that has been tenderized, combined with onions, tomatoes, and a generous amount of fresh coconut cream. The amalgamation of various textures and tastes is undeniably delectable.

D. 'Ufi 'Otai, also known as Baked Breadfruit, is a traditional dish that has cultural significance in certain regions.

Description: Ufi 'otai is a dish that consists of breadfruit slices that have been cooked until they reach a soft consistency. These slices are then accompanied with a coconut sauce that is both rich and creamy in texture. The culinary creation in question presents a harmonious combination of starch-based elements and the distinct flavor profile derived from coconut.

E. Ota 'Ika, also known as raw fish salad, is a traditional dish.

Description: Ota 'ika is Tonga's interpretation of the well recognized Polynesian culinary creation known as ceviche. The process involves immersing freshly caught fish in a mixture of coconut cream and lime juice, resulting in a vibrant and invigorating taste profile.

F. Fakakakai, also known as Tongan pastry, is a traditional culinary delicacy originating from the Kingdom of Tonga.

Description: Fakakakai refers to a kind of Tongan pastry that is crafted using a dough that has been sweetened. These pastries are often filled with pineapple jam or other similar sweet fillings. These delectable confections are savored on festive occasions.

In summary, the act of eating in Tonga extends beyond mere satiation of hunger, serving as a means to access the genuine warmth of Tongan hospitality and engage in a profound immersion inside the intricate fabric of Polynesian culture. The culinary experiences in Tonga include a diverse range of gastronomic delights, offering a captivating exploration of the South Pacific region. Whether one indulges in the delectable seafood options available along the coastal areas, partakes in the communal 'umu feast, or savors the delightful Tongan confections, each culinary encounter promises a rich and tasty immersion into the essence of Tongan cuisine.

THE END

Printed in Great Britain
by Amazon

40548488R00036